Space
A Look at Asteroids and Comets

Aaron Waldeck

The Rosen Publishing Group, Inc.
New York

Published in 2002 by The Rosen Publishing Group, Inc.
29 East 21st Street, New York, NY 10010

Book Design: Ron A. Churley

Photo Credits: Cover, pp. 1, 6–7 © Joe Tucciarone/Science Photo Library; p. 4 © Science Photo Library; p. 8 © Detlev Van Ravenswaay/Science Photo Library; pp. 11, 16–17 © Julian Baum/Photo Science Library; pp. 12–13 © John Foster/Science Source; p. 15 © Royal Greenwich Observatory/Science Photo Library/Photo Researchers, Inc.; p. 19 © Jerry Lodriguss/Photo Researchers, Inc., Photo Researchers, Inc.; pp. 20–21 © Pekka Parviainen/Science Photo Library; p. 22 © SuperStock.

ISBN: 0-8239-8235-1
6-pack ISBN: 0-8239-8638-1

Manufactured in the United States of America

Contents

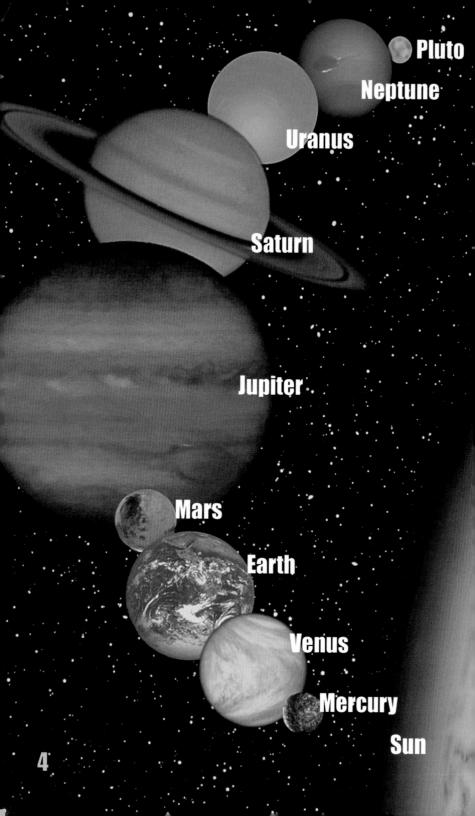

Pluto

Neptune

Uranus

Saturn

Jupiter

Mars

Earth

Venus

Mercury

Sun

4

Inside Our Solar System

We live on Earth, the third **planet** from the sun. The sun, Earth, eight other planets, and many moons make up our **solar system**. The planets and the moons of our solar system circle the sun because of a force called **gravity**.

Planets and moons are not the only objects that circle the sun. Asteroids and comets also circle the sun.

Mercury is the closest planet to the sun. Pluto is the farthest planet from the sun. Jupiter is the largest planet in our solar system.

What Are Asteroids?

Asteroids are rocks that **orbit** the sun. Asteroids are much smaller than planets, and they are not round like planets. They are bumpy and uneven. Most asteroids can be found in the space between Mars and Jupiter.

Scientists think that the moons orbiting some planets, such as Mars and Saturn, are actually large asteroids.

Some asteroids are so small we can't see them from Earth. The biggest asteroid we know of is as big as the state of Texas!

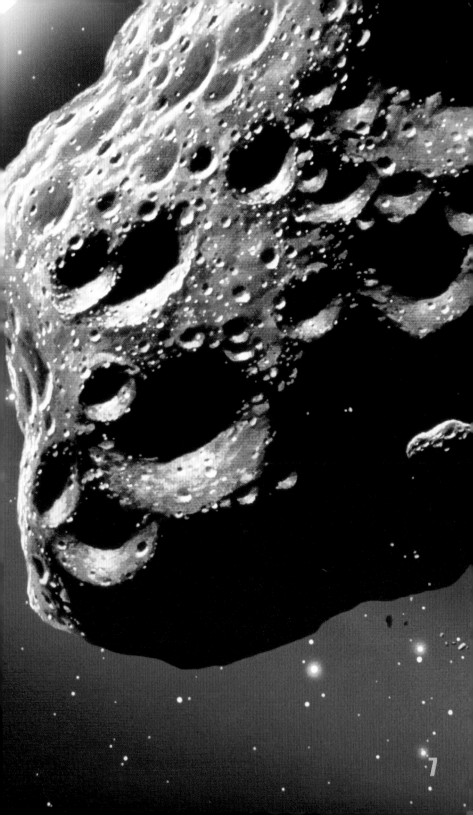

Asteroid Belt

What Is the Asteroid Belt?

Millions of asteroids form a ring between Mars and Jupiter. This ring, called the asteroid belt, orbits the sun. Sometimes these asteroids crash into each other and break into smaller asteroids.

Some scientists think the asteroid belt is what was left over after the sun and planets formed. Others believe that it is made up of planets that crashed into each other and were **destroyed** long ago.

If all the asteroids in the asteroid belt were put together, they would only be about half the size of Earth's moon.

Earth and Asteroids

The asteroid belt is not the only place in the solar system where there are asteroids. Scientists have found asteroids beyond Jupiter, and between Earth and the sun.

Some scientists believe an asteroid hit our planet about 65 million years ago, raising a huge dust cloud that blocked out sunlight and caused weather changes all over Earth. These weather changes may be the reason the dinosaurs died out.

An asteroid hit Earth about 65 million years ago. It left a crater about 190 miles wide off the eastern coast of Mexico!

What Are Comets?

Comets are balls of dust, ice, and gas that look like stars with tails. Comets also orbit the sun. They come very close to the sun, then travel farther out into the solar system.

Sometimes comets pass so close to Earth that we can see them in the sky for a few days or weeks. After they move on, we won't see them again for many years.

Comets are sometimes called "dirty snowballs" because they are made of ice and dust.

Parts of a Comet

The center of a comet is called the **nucleus**. The nucleus is made mostly of ice and frozen gas. This is the most solid part of a comet.

The nucleus gives off gases, dust, and water as it moves through the solar system. The gases, dust, and water form a cloud around the comet. This cloud is called the **coma**. The coma leaves a trail of dust behind it. This is called a tail.

We can see a comet's tail because light from the sun shines on it.

Tail

Coma

Nucleus

A Comet's Tail

The tail of a comet is the part we can see when a comet passes Earth. Heat from the sun causes part of the comet to melt. As the comet melts it gives off dust, which forms the comet's tail. Some tails can be

100 million miles long! A comet's tail always points away from the sun. This happens because sunlight pushes against the dust trail a comet leaves behind.

The word "comet" comes from the Greek word "*kometes,*" which means "long-haired."

A Famous Comet

In 1705, a scientist named Edmond Halley claimed that a comet that had passed Earth in 1682 would return in 1758. The comet did return, and it was named after Halley.

Halley's Comet passes near Earth about every 76 years. The last time Halley's Comet passed Earth was in 1986. Its next trip past Earth won't be until around 2061.

The first reports of Halley's Comet passing Earth were made by Chinese scientists over 2,200 years ago.

Edmond Halley

What Is a Meteor?

A meteor is a piece of a comet or asteroid that burns up as it falls to Earth. When many meteors fall to Earth at the same time, it is called a meteor shower.

Can you tell why meteors are sometimes called "falling stars" or "shooting stars"?

Halley's Comet leaves a long trail of dust and rock behind it as it passes through the solar system. Earth crosses this trail twice a year. The dust and rock enter our **atmosphere** and burn up as they fall to Earth, causing a meteor shower.

Learning More About Comets

In the last fifteen years, scientists have learned more about comets and asteroids by using **satellites** to study them. Scientists hope to study other comets and asteroids in the years to come.

In 1986, satellites from five countries followed Halley's Comet to study it up close.

Glossary

atmosphere The layer of air, gases, and dust that surrounds Earth.

coma A cloud of gas, dust, and water that surrounds a comet.

destroy To damage something so badly that it is gone forever.

gravity The force that causes planets, asteroids, and comets to circle the sun.

nucleus The center of a comet.

orbit To travel around another object in space. Earth orbits the sun, and the moon orbits Earth.

planet A large, round object that moves around the sun.

satellite A machine that travels through space used to study objects in our solar system.

scientist A person who studies the way things are and the way things act.

solar system The system made up of our sun, the nine planets, moons, and other space objects.

Index